DISCOVERING AMERICA
★ An Exceptional Nation ★

American Migration
and Settlement

Brett Griffin

Cavendish
Square

New York

Published in 2019 by Cavendish Square Publishing, LLC
243 5th Avenue, Suite 136, New York, NY 10016

Website: cavendishsq.com

This publication represents the opinions and views of the author based on his or her personal
experience, knowledge, and research. The information in this book serves as a general
guide only. The author and publisher have used their best efforts in preparing this book and
disclaim liability rising directly or indirectly from the use and application of this book.

All websites were available and accurate when this book was sent to press.

Cataloging-in-Publication Data

Names: Griffin, Brett.
Title: American migration and settlement / Brett Griffin.
Description: New York : Cavendish Square, 2019. | Series: Discovering
America: an exceptional nation | Includes glossary and index.
Identifiers: ISBN 9781502643131 (pbk.) | ISBN 9781502642653
(library bound) | ISBN 9781502643148 (ebook)
Subjects: LCSH: North America--Discovery and exploration--Juvenile literature. | United States-
-History--Colonial period, ca. 1600-1775--Juvenile literature. | United States--Emigration
and immigration--History--Juvenile literature. | Immigrants--United States--History--
Juvenile literature. | Migration, Internal--United States--History--Juvenile literature.
Classification: LCC E101.G75 2019 | DDC 970.01'2--dc23

Editorial Director: David McNamara
Editor: Caitlyn Miller
Copy Editor: Rebecca Rohan
Associate Art Director: Alan Sliwinski
Production Coordinator: Karol Szymczuk
Photo Research: J8 Media

Printed in the United States of America

CONTENTS

★   ★

Christopher Columbus arrived in the New World aboard the *Santa Maria* in 1492, beginning five centuries of migration to the Americas.

Chapter One

The Colonization of North America: 1492 to 1800

In the fall of 1492, three ships were sighted off the coast of an island in what is now the Bahamas. The island's inhabitants, mostly members of the indigenous Taíno tribe, hurried to meet the new arrivals on the beach. Led by Christopher Columbus, the voyagers were Spanish sailors tasked with finding a new route from Europe to the spice-rich East Indies. Initially thinking he had reached his destination, Columbus referred to the Natives he encountered as "Indians." The name stuck long after Columbus realized his mistake, and long after the Taíno people had been nearly wiped out. Columbus's voyage began centuries of migration and settlement in what would become the United States.

Columbus in the New World

Columbus was the first of many European explorers to the New World, and the results of his voyage were truly historic. The Columbian exchange of plants and animals changed the basic way of life on both sides of the Atlantic Ocean. New World crops like corn, potatoes, pumpkins, and tobacco were first introduced to Europe. Moving in the other direction, the practice of raising cattle, pigs, and horses was imported to the Americas. Unfortunately, life changed mostly for the worst for the Native Americans. Old World diseases accompanied the explorers and had devastating consequences for the Native population. The Europeans' desire for gold also wreaked havoc on the tribes of the Americas, beginning with Columbus's very first voyage.

The Taíno that greeted Columbus and his men were warm-hearted and welcoming, and Columbus was struck by their selflessness and sense of community. "When you ask for something they have," he wrote in a report to the Spanish monarchy that had sponsored his expedition, "they never say no. To the contrary, they offer to share with anyone." Columbus also noted that some Natives wore gold ornaments in their ears and that none possessed firearms. Together, these observations led him to conclude that the seemingly primitive Natives could be easily taken as servants or slaves and forced to reveal the sources of their gold. Columbus captured ten Taíno Natives to bring back to Spain and demonstrate the possibility of such a project. Though several died aboard the ship during the journey, enough survived that a return trip was financed. Seventeen ships were sent back to the Caribbean with 1,200 men, on a mission to round up Native slaves and acquire as much gold as possible.

The behavior of the Europeans during this mission took a heavy toll on the Natives of the Caribbean. Epidemics of smallpox, plague, and yellow fever broke out almost immediately and were incredibly deadly. Since the Natives had never been exposed to these diseases before, they had no resistance to them and died in droves. In addition to disease, the imprisonment and enslavement of the Natives also led to mass deaths. Native slaves died by the hundreds aboard ships bound for Spain. Thousands more were worked to death in the Caribbean, searching for gold that in many cases did not exist. On the island of Hispaniola (present-day Haiti and the Dominican Republic), Native slaves were told to collect a certain amount of gold every three months. Those that failed to meet their quotas (usually because there simply was not such a quantity of gold to be found) had their hands cut off and were left to bleed to death. Many Natives fled these conditions and were hunted down and killed. Others committed

Upon his arrival in the Caribbean, Christopher Columbus was fascinated by the friendliness of the Natives he encountered. Writing to the king and queen of Spain, he reported that the Natives "love their neighbors as themselves, and their discourse is ever sweet and gentle, and accompanied with a smile; and though it is true that they are naked, yet their manners are decorous and praiseworthy."

Similar first impressions were made on later explorers and settlers. Europeans were usually warmly greeted upon first contact. They made note of how friendly, self-sufficient, and supportive Native communities were of one another. Some white settlers ran off to join the Natives. During the French and Indian War in the mid-eighteenth century, a group of white children captured by a Native tribe refused to return to their parents after the war was over. They preferred the Native society over that of their own people. This caused Hector St. John de Crèvecoeur, a Frenchman living in the American colonies at the time, to say, "There must be in [the Natives'] social bond, something singularly captivating, and far superior to anything to be boasted among us; for thousands of Europeans are Indians, and we have no example of even one of those Aborigines having from choice become Europeans."

suicide in large groups, knowing that resistance against the superior weapons of the Spanish was futile. Within two years of Columbus's arrival on Hispaniola, half of the island's 250,000 Natives were dead. By the mid-sixteenth century, more than 90 percent of the Taíno population of the lands supposedly "discovered" by Columbus had been wiped out.

Columbus's actions after arriving in the New World were unfortunately typical. Believing himself naturally superior to the Natives, Columbus felt that he and his fellow Europeans were entitled to the wealth of the New World. This attitude of racial superiority, combined with a never-ending desire for ever more land and wealth, would go on to shape the next four centuries of migration to, and settlement in, the Americas.

The Planting of the American Colonies

The history of migration to what is now the United States began with the founding of the English colonies along the Atlantic coast of North America. The English population had boomed in the second half of the sixteenth century, increasing from three to four million in just fifty years. This resulted in increasing unemployment and a growing number of people who lacked the means to support

The first English settlers of the Jamestown colony only survived by trading with local Native American tribes.

themselves. At the same time, English primogeniture laws, which made the firstborn son of a family the heir to the family's lands, titles, and wealth, produced a class of second and third sons. These men, though not themselves poor, nevertheless had limited prospects in England. Both of these groups saw the New World as a place where they could lead a better life. Those with money formed joint stock companies, in which multiple investors pooled their resources to fund expeditions to the Americas. Those without money signed up for the expeditions as sailors or servants.

In 1607, the Virginia Company chartered the Jamestown colony, the first permanent English settlement in North America. Jamestown, and later the entire colony of Virginia, was formed with the intention of finding gold. The initial settlers numbered about one hundred. Many of them had no experience with farming or agriculture and began digging for gold immediately upon arrival rather than looking for food. As a result, the first settlers in Jamestown died in large numbers from disease or starvation. The winter of 1609–1610 was known as the "starving time," as settlers eventually resorted to cannibalism to stay alive. During the first three years of the colony's existence, 500 people died. By 1625, more than 6,000 of the first 7,200 settlers had perished. An uneasy alliance with local Native American tribes helped the colony get on its feet, proving that it was possible to establish settlements in the New World.

By the start of the American Revolution in 1775, there were thirteen colonies in total, all formed at different times for different reasons by different groups of people. Maryland was founded as a haven for Catholics, who were a religious minority in England. Though Protestant settlers eventually came to outnumber Catholics in the Maryland colony, a local ordinance granted all Christians equality under the law. The Carolinas were chartered largely to provide food for European settlements in the Caribbean and eventually became the breadbasket of the American colonies. Georgia, the last of the Southern colonies, was initially imagined of as a place where those owing money in England could go to work off their debts and eventually start over. Settlers throughout the Southern colonies had to deal with the unhealthy living conditions of the region. The climate allowed disease to spread quickly, especially around the Chesapeake Bay, and made it hard for settlers to raise families. Most colonists were men in their late teens or early twenties, and they initially outnumbered female colonists six to one. Even by 1700, men still accounted for 60 percent of the region's population. Families were not very common, and those that did exist often saw one partner die within seven years.

New England and the Middle Colonies

By contrast, settlers in New England had a higher life expectancy than they would have had even in England. The first settlers to arrive in New England were the Pilgrims, separatists from the Church of England who had originally intended to land in the Virginia colony. Going off course and arriving at Plymouth Rock aboard the *Mayflower* instead, the Pilgrims began living there in 1620. The colony at Plymouth eventually merged with the larger (and legally chartered) Massachusetts Bay Colony, which had been founded by more moderate Puritans in 1630. Both the Puritans and the Pilgrims left England over disagreements with the doctrine of the Church of England, the Pilgrims fearing for their safety if they continued to stay in their native country. In the New World, they envisioned a colony that could serve as "a city upon a hill," a shining example of the wonders of Puritan Protestantism. More than twenty thousand Puritans came to Massachusetts between 1630 and 1640, including many families. As the population grew, the colony began to expand beyond the bounds of the initial charter. New colonies were created as a result, including Connecticut and New Hampshire.

Religious freedom motivated the seeding of other colonies as well. Rhode Island was settled in 1636 by Roger Williams. He had found the religious zeal of Massachusetts too overbearing and wanted to live in a community that was more tolerant of religious diversity. The colony of Pennsylvania had similar origins. From its beginnings in 1681, the colony was intended by its founder, William Penn, to be a haven for members of the Religious Society of Friends, or Quakers. Pennsylvania was unique among the colonies for several reasons, not least of which was its tolerance for other religions (though neither Catholics nor Jews could vote or hold elected office). The colony also maintained a peaceful attitude toward the Native American tribes and had a clear distaste for slavery.

The so-called middle colonies represented something of a blending of the colonies of New England and those of the South. New York had initially been founded as New Netherland by the Dutch, who "bought" the island of Manhattan from the Natives and immediately constructed a wall around it to prevent attacks. They also drove out the initial Swedish settlers of Delaware before they were themselves forced to surrender their territories to the British. New Jersey was later formed from parts of both New York and Pennsylvania. The middle colonies contained more agricultural land than New England, but nothing to rival the farmlands of the South. They were also more reliant on industry than their Southern neighbors.

Indentured Servitude

While some settlers came to the colonies in search of religious freedom and others came seeking economic opportunities, more than half of those who came to North America in the colonial period were indentured servants. Indentured servants sold their labor to a master in the colonies for a set period of time in exchange for paid passage across the Atlantic and "freedom dues" when their term of indenture was up (contracts usually lasted between five and seven years). Freedom dues consisted of corn, money, and, for men, a piece of land. This appealed to the English (and later Irish and German) poor, who were increasingly struggling in overcrowded cities.

Indentured servitude at least offered a chance of someday gaining land and possibly wealth, which was enough to convince many Europeans to deal with the miserable conditions that came with the job. Servants' rights were restricted by their masters, and they were often beaten when they were thought to not be working hard enough. Female indentured servants were regularly subjected to sexual assault. In the early years of the Southern colonies, indentured servants were the primary labor force on plantations established in the hot and disease-ridden climate of the Chesapeake. As a

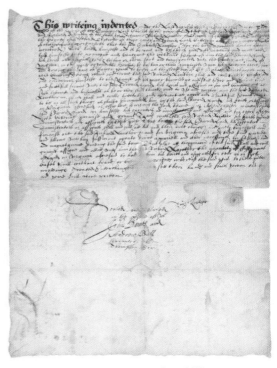

A contract for indentured servitude from 1627

result of these conditions, when the period of indenture was finished, 80 percent of servants were either dead, back in England, or living in poverty. Very few ever managed to prosper in the American colonies. More than one hundred thousand indentured servants came to North America before 1700. As working conditions in England changed at the turn of the century, the numbers of prospective servants dropped. Southern planters were still desperately in need of labor, however, and began turning increasingly to African slaves to meet their demand.

The Involuntary Migrants

The European use of Africans as slaves began in the late fifteenth century, when Portuguese traders bought slaves for use on sugar plantations established off the continent's Atlantic coast. Over the next two centuries, African slavery became an institution in the New World, especially in South America and the Caribbean. The Natives that had initially been enslaved by Columbus and his peers had not served the purpose the Europeans had in mind for them. Vast numbers were killed by diseases, and those that survived were far more familiar with the lands where they had been born than their European masters. This familiarity allowed them to successfully escape and find shelter with other members of their tribe. Natives also lacked many skills that Europeans were hoping for in their slave laborers, particularly the ability to raise livestock. African slaves, by contrast, came from societies with horses and cattle and knew how to properly care for animals. They were also more resistant to European diseases and were utter strangers in the New World. There was nowhere for them to run or find sanctuary.

African men, women, and children were captured in the interior of the continent, lashed together, and marched to the coast at gunpoint. Around 40 percent died during these forced marches. On the coast, the prisoners were held in cages and inspected by slavers before they were purchased and transported across the Atlantic. Conditions on the slave ships were miserable. Slaves were packed into cramped holds below-decks, often chained together, lying prone in a space only 18 inches (46 centimeters) in height. On the average ship, 20 to 35 percent of the slaves died before reaching the Americas. Many threw themselves overboard if presented with the opportunity, choosing death over bondage. The survivors were sold on auction blocks in the New World and became the property of their

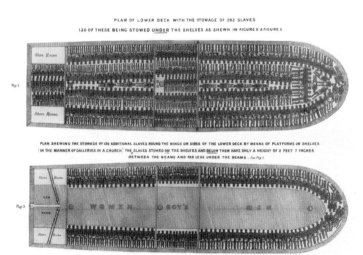

Captive Africans endured miserably cramped conditions in the slave ships that brought them across the Atlantic to be sold as slaves in the New World.

purchasers. From 1500 to 1800, somewhere between ten and fifteen million Africans were transported as slaves to the Americas. Including those that died in Africa or on the trip across the Atlantic, the African continent lost a total of nearly fifty million people to death or slavery in those three hundred years.

The first slaves arrived in Virginia in 1619. Though they were initially too expensive for most settlers to afford, as time went on that situation changed. The Southern colonies, which depended on the cultivation of tobacco for their wealth, needed labor. At first, indentured servants were contracted to perform work on tobacco plantations. As the supply of servants began to dry up in the late seventeenth century, however, Southern planters began turning to African slaves to fill the void. Slaves cost more initially but were cheaper in the long run. Slaves were under no contract, masters had no obligation to provide anything to them, and they had no legal right to seek their liberty. Slavery was even made inheritable—the child of a slave was also considered a slave. By the time of the American Revolution, slavery formed the economic basis of life in all thirteen colonies. Even in New England, where slavery did not exist in any significant quantity because of the lack of large-scale agriculture, banks made their money off of the slave trade, insurance companies existed to provide coverage for slave ships, and other industries (fisheries, rum distilleries, etc.) profited off trade with slave colonies in the Caribbean. In this way, the wealth of the American colonies was built on the backs of imported African slave labor.

By 1750, black slaves accounted for half the population of Virginia. In South Carolina, there were twice as many slaves as free white settlers. In all, by the time the slave trade was outlawed in 1808, four hundred thousand Africans had been brought to the American colonies. These population numbers led to the development of a unique African American culture among the slaves, who were often members of different tribes with different customs, thrown together in the colonies. The population difference between colonists and slaves also led to the development of slave codes, which were designed to keep slaves in line and prevent them from rising up and rebelling against their white masters. In many places, slaves were forbidden from learning to read or write. Masters were permitted to inflict brutal punishments for any acts of resistance or escape attempts. Blacks were also said to be inferior in all ways to whites, in an effort to destroy any potential cooperation between slaves and poor whites. If black slaves and white servants attempted to escape together, the slaves received much harsher punishments. Freedom dues for indentured servants were also increased, and intermarriage and other forms of relationships between whites and blacks were forbidden. These were all deliberate efforts by the planters to prevent any sense of community between the slaves and their lower-class white neighbors, who might otherwise band together against the wealthy Southern elite.

The Victims of Colonization

At the same time that slavery was being established as a crucial part of the colonial economy, the settlers in America were pushing westward. Those making the push were seeking more land on which to build plantations, farms, or towns. As had happened since the arrival of the first Europeans, this brought the colonists into conflict with the Native American inhabitants of those regions. The popular image of colonists hacking a life for themselves out of hostile wilderness is a myth. That myth erases the fact that, before Columbus arrived in the Caribbean in 1492, anywhere from seventy-five million to one hundred million people already lived in the Americas. Though exact population figures are difficult to come by, scholars generally agree that there were fifteen million Natives living in present-day Canada and the United States at the time of Columbus's arrival. The Natives were divided into hundreds of tribes, each with their own unique religions, languages, and customs. The tribes practiced complex agriculture, raising a much wider variety of vegetables than were grown in Europe at the time and using crop rotation systems to replenish nutrients in the soil. Organized settlements were home to up to ten thousand inhabitants. The city of Cahokia, near present-day St. Louis, Missouri, contained nearly forty thousand people. Lands were shared among members of the tribe, women were held in high esteem and performed crucial roles in village life, and children were raised by the community to make the most of their potential. Though tribes often fought with one another, alliances were not unheard of. The Iroquois Confederacy in what is now the state of New York is the clearest example of several tribes working together to achieve general prosperity and security.

The advancements of the Natives were no match for the guns of the Europeans, however, and there was no defense for the diseases that were brought to the New World in explorers' ships. The great Aztec and Inca civilizations of Central and South America were systematically wiped out by Spanish conquistadores, whose greed for gold and glory knew no bounds. The Native population of present-day Mexico shrank from twenty million to two million in less than a century. Those not killed outright were taken as slaves and eventually worked to death in mines. Attempts to fight back were crushed because the weapons of the Europeans were able to easily overpower Native resistance. Waves of disease epidemics also ravaged Native communities across both continents throughout the sixteenth and seventeenth centuries, with mortality rates from smallpox, measles, plague, cholera, and typhoid as high as 75 percent in some tribes. Serious epidemics struck the Native tribes at roughly four-year intervals, killing thousands of men, women, and children each time.

The English settlers took advantage of the disease-weakened state of North American tribes to establish their colonies and push deeper into the continent's interior. The initial colonists in both Virginia and Massachusetts owed their survival in the first years of settlement to the Native tribes that helped them plant and grow food. However, they did not hesitate to turn on their neighbors when their presence became inconvenient to the further growth of the colony. The Jamestown settlers began stealing food from the local Powhatan tribes when their own crops proved slow to grow, prompting the Powhatan to fight back and attempt to drive the colonists out of the region.

In 1622, after an attack that resulted in the deaths of five hundred colonists, the Virginia Company called for "a perpetual war" designed to prevent the Powhatan "from being any longer a people." Native villages were burned to the ground, food supplies were destroyed, and Natives were massacred during what were supposed to be peace talks. By 1669, 90 percent of the Native population of Virginia had been killed. In New England, the Pequot tribe was wiped out during a war in the 1630s, and King Philip's War

King Philip's War

Without the help of the Natives of New England, the first colonists would have struggled to survive in the region. Epidemics of disease had taken a heavy toll on the Wampanoag and Narragansett tribes of modern-day Massachusetts and Connecticut. However, surviving members of the tribes offered to help the Pilgrims and Puritans plant crops and adapt to their new home. This friendliness decreased as increasing numbers of settlers arrived in the new colonies and began pushing into Native lands. By the 1670s, there were fifty-two thousand colonists and just ten thousand Natives, which prompted the Wampanoag chief Metacom to forge a confederacy of tribes in the region. Dubbed "King Philip" by the English in an effort to win his loyalty through flattery, Metacom was determined to resist further encroachments by the whites.

War began in 1675, and though the Natives had some initial successes, by the spring of 1676, the tide had turned against them. Disease, food shortages, and massacres of civilians by the colonial militias had taken their toll, and the Natives were forced to surrender. Five thousand Natives had died, and two thousand more fled the region. The colonists had lost eight hundred people, and seventeen villages had been destroyed by Metacom's confederacy. Metacom himself was captured and executed. Both the Wampanoag and the Narragansett tribes were virtually wiped out.

The thirteen English colonies that would eventually revolt against the Crown and declare their independence

of 1675–1676 brought about the end of the Wampanoag and the Narragansett. Both wars involved the deliberate massacres of Native women and children, in an effort to force the Natives to give up and abandon their lands. John Winthrop, the governor of the Massachusetts Bay Colony, justified the violence by claiming that the Natives had not "improved" the lands of North America and that the colonists therefore had a God-given right to them. These claims were false, but they continued to influence American policy toward the Native Americans for centuries to come. In total, in the time between Columbus's arrival in 1492 and the American Revolution in the late eighteenth century, more than 90 percent of the Native population that had once lived north of the Rio Grande had been destroyed.

At the same time, the white and black populations boomed. There were three hundred thousand people in the colonies in 1700. By 1775, that number had climbed to 2.5 million. Over the same period, twenty thousand black slaves grew into half a million. In several Southern colonies, slaves accounted for 50 percent or more of the total population. The white population was overwhelmingly

English in origin, though minority communities of Germans and Scots-Irish lived on the western frontier. This frontier, established along the Appalachian Mountains, was created by the Royal Proclamation of 1763. The proclamation forbade settlement west of the mountains "on Pain of [Royal] displeasure" after white encroachments in the Ohio valley had prompted a Native revolt. Led by an Ottawa chief known as Pontiac, the rebellion had been successfully repressed, partially through the deliberate distribution of smallpox-infected blankets to the Natives. It had also convinced the British government of the necessity of limiting its American colonies to the coast, in order to prevent further conflict with the Natives before their land could be legally taken.

The proclamation had financial consequences for many of the Founding Fathers, as George Washington, Thomas Jefferson, and James Madison, among others, had speculative investments in western lands. The British government had now become an obstacle to gaining further wealth in the colonies, and the first steps along the road to revolution had been taken. Other outrages over the next decade would lead to a war for independence. At the end of the American Revolution, the disputed lands between the Appalachians and the Mississippi River were granted to the newly independent colonies, allowing the next phase of American expansion to begin.

Meriwether Lewis and William Clark explored the lands of the Louisiana Purchase, the first major expansion in the history of the United States.

★ Chapter Two ★

Manifest Destiny and Westward Expansion: 1800 to 1877

In 1790, only 5 percent of the population of the newly independent United States lived west of the Appalachian Mountains. By 1850, the country stretched from the Atlantic to the Pacific Ocean, and the population had spread throughout the continent. This rapid expansion was accompanied by a feeling among many Americans that it was God's desire that the population spread their civilized, democratic, Christian ideals into the "heathen" wilderness. It was a variation on John Winthrop's idea of two centuries earlier that the colonists needed to "improve" the land of the Natives. Newspaper editor John O'Sullivan gave the phenomenon a name in 1845. O'Sullivan wrote that it was Americans' "manifest destiny to overspread the continent allotted by Providence for the free development of our yearly multiplying millions." Manifest destiny brought about the expansion of the United States from coast to coast. It also led to a war with Mexico, the destruction of the remaining Native tribes within the country's borders, and, ultimately, the Civil War.

Manifest Destiny

Before the term "manifest destiny" had even been coined, the United States was already growing in size. The Louisiana Purchase of 1803 had added the lands between the Mississippi River and the Rocky Mountains to the country. Florida was also "purchased" in 1819, though no money changed hands. Instead, Spain agreed to cede the territory after Andrew Jackson invaded with an army to suppress Native revolts. In return, the American government promised to respect Spanish claims to Texas. These claims proved short-lived, as Mexico, of which Texas was part, gained its independence in 1821. A group of American settlers led by Stephen Austin made arrangements with the Mexican government to migrate there, but the slaves they brought to the region soon put them in violation of Mexican law. (Mexico had abolished slavery in 1829.) As a result, Texas declared its independence in 1836. The United States was at first hesitant to annex

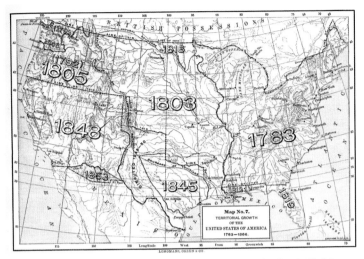

The United States expanded in several stages throughout the first half of the nineteenth century, shown by the dates of territorial acquisitions on this map.

Texas, despite the clear signals that Texans longed to be added to the Union. Then James Polk was elected to the presidency in 1844 on an explicitly expansionist platform. At that point, outgoing president John Tyler annexed the territory, hoping to add the Lone Star state to his legacy.

When Polk took office in 1845, manifest destiny was at its height. Polk had two goals for expansion. First, he negotiated with Great Britain to gain the Oregon Country of the Pacific Northwest in 1846. Second, he attempted to purchase California from Mexico. Still furious about the annexation of Texas, which they considered illegal, the Mexican government refused to sell. Polk, believing that the United States had a divine right to any land it desired, opted to take California by force. He dispatched General Zachary Taylor to the border between Texas and Mexico with instructions to provoke a war. Taylor's troops entered territory to which the United States had no clear claim. When Mexican soldiers opened fire on soldiers they believed to be illegally invading their country, the president declared that American blood had been spilled on American soil and that the United States had been attacked. Congress overwhelmingly went along with the charade, declaring war almost unanimously. The Mexican-American War lasted from 1846 to 1848. At its conclusion, the United States had gained not only Texas and California, but all the lands between—half of Mexico's pre-war territory. The United States paid the Mexican government a little over $15 million (roughly $450 million in today's dollars), but this was merely meant to provide cover for what was otherwise a very obvious war of conquest.

With the Mexican Cession of 1848 and the Gadsden Purchase of a small stretch of land in the Southwest in 1853, the continental United States was complete. Settlers began spreading out across the vast new territories added to the country, aided by new transportation technologies. Roads, steamboats, and canals made travel around the eastern United States easier. The explosion of railroad construction in the 1850s began speeding migration to the new lands in the West.

Life on the western frontier was not easy. Food was scarce, dwellings were poorly built, and frontiersmen often died of disease. Still, land was cheap, and eastern cities had become crowded. Not only was the native-born American population growing throughout the nineteenth century, but new immigrants continued to arrive on the country's shores.

Immigration and Its Discontents

Though thousands of immigrants came to the United States every year, the first major immigration boom in the nation's history took place from 1840 to 1860. During those twenty years, more than three million immigrants arrived in the country, the vast majority of them from Germany and Ireland. The Irish came to America following a potato blight that had resulted in the deaths of two million people. Most arrived with little money and lived in cities in extremely poor conditions. The Irish accounted for half of all immigration in the 1840s. German immigrants fled not only crop failures but also political turmoil. Revolutions in the mid-nineteenth century prompted many Germans to leave their homeland and make the transatlantic voyage. Usually possessing more money than the Irish, German immigrants settled in large numbers on farms and in cities in the American Midwest, where German culture mingled with American culture. Immigrants from elsewhere in Northern and Western Europe, including Great Britain, Denmark, and Sweden, also came to the United States in this period, but not in numbers anywhere near those of the Irish and Germans.

There was a backlash to these immigrants, particularly against the Irish. American nativists feared that immigrants would outbreed, outvote, and eventually replace the "native" population. (The fact that those raising this objection were themselves not native to the Americas and had forcibly removed or exterminated the actual Natives went unmentioned.) Protestants distrusted the Catholic Irish immigrants and resented that newcomers were "stealing" jobs. A new political party, the American Party (also referred to as the "Know-Nothing" Party), was formed to run on an exclusively xenophobic platform. (Xenophobia is the dislike or distrust of foreigners.) The party sought restrictions on immigration, deportations of poor immigrants, and to limit the holding of political office to native-born Americans. Nativists also took part in violence against immigrants, including the burning of Catholic churches. The Know-Nothings ran former president Millard Fillmore in the presidential election of 1856, but he only carried the state of Maryland. The party folded shortly thereafter. The Irish continued to face discrimination for decades, until second- and third-

In response to anti-Irish discrimination, particularly "No Irish Need Apply" signs posted on American and British businesses, Irish émigrés sang songs in protest, including this popular number first published in 1862.

generation Irish-Americans managed to accumulate enough wealth and property to gain access to the upper classes of American society—and to political office.

The Removal of the Native Americans

By 1830, the population of the United States had swelled to thirteen million. Most lands east of the Mississippi River had at this point been admitted to the Union as states. The surviving Native population of the region was stranded in the midst of a sea of whites. There were 120,000 Natives living between the Mississippi and the Appalachian Mountains in 1820. By 1844, fewer than thirty thousand remained. The Natives who had lived in those lands (or who had been forced into those lands by the presence of the original colonies) were removed to make room for further white settlements and to allow for the spread of the Cotton Kingdom in the South and the construction of railways, canals, and cities in the North. As had been the case in the colonial era, the Natives were only allowed to live on their lands in peace if it was convenient for the whites. When settlers or planters decided they needed more land, they simply took it, believing themselves naturally entitled to any land on the continent, regardless of the presence of Native residents. A series of Supreme Court decisions by Chief Justice John Marshall in the early nineteenth century essentially turned this attitude into federal law, making it effectively illegal for Native tribes to do anything to resist white encroachment. American settlers could quite literally never be in the wrong in their dealings with the Natives because those Natives were not citizens and were not deemed to have any rights that had to be respected. Though Marshall recommended that treaties signed with Native tribes still be followed where possible, his rulings made it clear that no treaty-breaking on the part of the American government would ever be punished.

The promise made in the Northwest Ordinance of 1787 that "[Natives'] land property shall never be taken from them without their consent" was swiftly broken in the years following it, as settlers crossed the Appalachians and began taking possession of lands that had not been ceded by the Natives. The Treaty of Grenville, signed in 1795, had reserved certain lands in the Ohio River valley for the region's tribes. Settlers ignored the treaty's terms, however, and continued to push forward into the territory. The federal government did not enforce the treaty's provisions, prompting several tribes to unite under a leader known as Tecumseh. A member of the Shawnee tribe, Tecumseh pointedly asked, "Where today are the Pequot? Where are the Narragansett ... and many other once powerful tribes of our people? They have vanished before the avarice and oppression of the White Man, as snow before a summer sun." Tecumseh's confederacy fought to avoid the fate of the tribes of the coast, but they were overwhelmed by the superior military might of the United States. Future

L ong before he became president, Andrew Jackson gained a reputation as one of the fiercest foes of the Native Americans in the United States. Though he was later

Andrew Jackson was a brutal enemy of the Native Americans during his time in the US military, and his anti-Native beliefs were made law during his presidency.

credited with representing the interests of the "common man," Jackson was in reality a Tennessee aristocrat, owning a massive plantation and more than one hundred slaves. He also developed a hatred for Native Americans, whose presence affected his land investments along the frontier. Jackson led several campaigns against the Natives while serving in the army. He dealt brutally with his enemies. In one encounter with rebels from the Creek tribe in 1813, Jackson promised his men that they could keep any property taken from the Natives they killed, to encourage them to be as ruthless as possible. At the Battle of Horseshoe Bend in 1814, Jackson took on an army of one thousand Creek warriors. He and his men killed eight hundred of them and secured the cession of half of the Creek nation's lands in a treaty following the battle.

Jackson also led troops in the Seminole War in Florida. Though it was still a Spanish territory at the time, Jackson nonetheless launched raids into the region in 1819, burning Seminole villages and seizing Spanish forts out of which his soldiers could operate. Jackson's presence was a major contributor to the Spanish decision to cede Florida to the United States later that year. He was rewarded for his efforts with an appointment to serve as the first military governor of the newly acquired territory.

president William Henry Harrison led the soldiers that shattered the confederacy at the Battle of Tippecanoe in 1811. Tecumseh died fighting alongside the British in the War of 1812. Native resistance in the Ohio River valley died with him. Finally, the short-lived Black Hawk War of 1832 led to the defeat of the Sauk and Fox tribes of Illinois and Wisconsin, clearing the way for white settlement throughout the Midwest.

The situation was slightly different in the South. Though many Natives were forced to cede their lands to white settlers through bribery or threat of violence, other tribes were encouraged to adopt the traditions and practices of the whites in order to keep their lands. These attempts to "civilize" the Natives were meant to eliminate any unique aspect of Native culture and make them indistinguishable from whites. These tactics destroyed tribal solidarity and made it easier to convince the tribes to open their lands to settlement. Many tribes went along with these initiatives, in a good faith effort to placate the US government and avoid extermination. The Cherokee in particular made a concerted effort to become "civilized," adopting notions of private property, developing a written alphabet, welcoming Christian missionaries, and even purchasing black slaves. It still was not enough.

Following the election of the notoriously anti-Native Andrew Jackson as president in 1828, state laws in Mississippi, Alabama, and Georgia dissolved the tribes within their borders as legal entities and opened their lands to white settlement. The discovery of gold on Cherokee land in Georgia only sped up the process of invasion. Bits of land began to be sold by desperate Natives. In 1830, Jackson signed the Indian Removal Act into law. This legislation called for the forced migration of all Native peoples east of the Mississippi River to the Indian Territory (present-day Oklahoma), where the Natives were told they would be left alone for "as long as grass grows or water runs." Over the next decade, more than seventy thousand Natives were forcibly removed from the lands of their birth and driven west. Attempts at resistance failed. The Seminole fought a long war in Florida but were outlasted by the American military. A missionary sued on behalf of the Cherokee, and though the Supreme Court surprisingly ruled in favor of the tribe, Jackson refused to enforce the ruling. Beginning in the fall of 1838, fifteen thousand Cherokee were marched at gunpoint on a 116-day journey to the Indian Territory. Four thousand died of exposure, disease, or starvation along what came to be known as the Trail of Tears. The removal of the tribes also led to the deaths of half the population of the Creek and Seminole peoples.

Driven westward like cattle, four thousand Cherokee died during their forced removal from their homes in Georgia.

Manifest Destiny and the Civil War

As the United States expanded across the continent during the nineteenth century, slavery became an increasingly contentious issue between the North and the South. Slavery had been abolished in Northern states at the same time that it had exploded in Southern states. The invention of the cotton gin in 1793 revolutionized cotton production. Cotton came to replace tobacco as *the* cash crop of the South in the early 1800s. Factories in New England and Europe relied on Southern cotton for their textile manufacturing. By 1860, over 1 million tons (907,185 tonnes) were being produced per year. The demand for slave labor to work the cotton plantations increased over the same period, until by 1860 there were four million slaves in the United States. As slaveholders moved into new territories, they took their slaves with them. The presence or absence of large numbers of slaves typically determined whether a territory would enter the Union as a slave state or a free state.

Southern planters were anxious to preserve the balance of slave states and free states, so that they would be assured equal representation in Congress and antislavery laws could be voted down. As new states joined the Union, however, antislavery advocates became determined to prevent the expansion of slavery outside of the South. The Missouri Compromise of 1820 temporarily preserved the balance and forbade slavery north of latitude 36°30'. However, further acquisitions of land proved how ineffective this was as a long-term solution. The Mexican Cession added vast swaths of new territory to the country. Proslavery voices argued that the residents of these territories should decide for themselves whether or not to allow slavery, even in territories north of the compromise line, in line with the principles of popular sovereignty (or rule by the people). The discovery of gold in California, meanwhile, had sparked a rush of miners to the region, followed by laundry workers, restaurateurs, and hoteliers looking to make money off the prospectors. The sudden swelling of the population brought lawlessness. Concerns about maintaining order prompted calls for faster admission of California to the Union, in order to have a more functional government to enforce laws.

Southern slave owners saw the writing on the wall. California's drafted constitution outlawed slavery, and slaves had not been brought in large numbers into any of the territories gained from Mexico. Though the Compromise of 1850 included measures designed to accommodate Southern interests (opening the Mexican Cession territories outside of California to popular sovereignty and a new, harsher Fugitive Slave Law), the Southern ruling class was still not satisfied. They felt certain that the balance was tilting permanently in favor of the free states. Growing desperate, Southern politicians insisted on the passage of the Kansas and Nebraska Acts of 1854, which opened even more territory to popular sovereignty and further motivated the abolitionists. Southerners also began looking to expand into the Caribbean, to acquire more territories that could enter the Union as slave states. A lone man launched an invasion of Nicaragua and proclaimed himself the president of a new, pro-slavery republic. He was quickly overthrown and executed. The island of Cuba was also

In March 1857, the Supreme Court issued its judgement in the case of *Dred Scott v. Sandford*. Scott, a slave, had sued his master for his freedom after being taken to Illinois and the Wisconsin Territory, both lands where slavery was illegal. Scott's case was supported by abolitionists, but the Supreme Court's ruling was not in their favor. Chief Justice Roger Taney

Dred Scott was a slave who sued for his freedom, and the case had major repercussions.

first declared that Dred Scott lacked the ability to sue in federal courts, as he was a slave and not a citizen. Taney went on to rule that because slaves were legally considered property and not people, they could be transported into any territory, slave or free, and remain under the control of their masters. This was a fundamentally new interpretation of the law. It made the Missouri Compromise unconstitutional and effectively legalized slavery throughout the entire country. Slaveholders were emboldened by the decision, abolitionists were outraged, and the country moved one step closer to the Civil War.

This nineteenth-century engraving depicts a typical, though caricatured, pre–Civil War cotton plantation.

targeted by Southern politicians. In 1854, a secret manifesto was drawn up proposing an offer to buy the island from the Spanish, with contingency plans for an invasion if the offer was refused. The manifesto leaked before the plans could be implemented, however, and Northern outrage forced those in favor to back down.

The determination of the Southern planter class to keep their slaves, and with them their way of economic and social life, was beyond compromise by 1860. It could only be settled by force. The Civil War of 1861 to 1865 claimed the lives of more than seven hundred thousand people and fundamentally reshaped American society. Though many factors combined to push the slavery crisis to the point of war, the desire for more land, shown in the idea of manifest destiny, was one of the most important. The addition of so much new territory to the Union made it impossible to ignore the horrors of slavery, which threatened to get worse if slavery was allowed to expand further. The casualties of the Civil War, together with those of the Mexican-American War and the thousands of Native Americans exterminated during removal efforts, represent the human cost of the westward expansion of the United States.

Immigrants arrive at Ellis Island at the turn of the twentieth century, part of an immigration boom that brought millions to America's shores.

★ Chapter Three ★

Immigration and Exclusion: 1877 to 1945

I n 1860, there were thirty-one million people living in the United States. By 1900, that number had grown to eighty million. Over the same period, America's cities had tripled in size, with 40 percent of Americans living in urban areas at the turn of the twentieth century. The move to the cities was closely tied to the country's increasing industrial capacity, which was in turn spurred on by the explosion in railroads in the years following the Civil War. The federal government granted lands in the western territories to railroad companies, in an effort to subsidize the growth of the industry. As a result, the 35,000 miles (56,300 kilometers) of track in the country in 1865 had expanded to 192,500 miles (310,000 km) in 1900. These railroads opened up markets across the country and allowed workers and raw materials to travel to new settlements out west.

The Dawn of the Industrial Revolution

The ease of transport of both people and goods fanned the flames of the Industrial Revolution. Steel, oil, and electricity came to dominate the country at the end of the nineteenth century and allowed captains of industry to accumulate wealth in quantities previously unheard of. As these industries prospered, opportunities for employment became plentiful, attracting immigrants and native-born Americans to the cities where factories and processing plants were located. Electric lights allowed cities to operate around the clock. Electric streetcars (and later automobiles) made it possible for cities to expand outward without increasing the commute time of workers. The rapid growth of major cities like New York, Chicago, and Philadelphia led to overcrowding and miserable living conditions for many of the new arrivals. Poor workers and immigrants were packed together in small, cramped tenements or slums, with entire families sometimes being forced to share one tiny room.

New York City, 1900. Cities attracted increasing numbers of native-born Americans and immigrants during the late nineteenth and early twentieth centuries.

Among the migrants to the cities were those African Americans who had the means to travel out of the South. The Civil War had resulted in the freeing of the slaves, but the period of Reconstruction following the war was ended before the black population could be properly integrated into Southern society. Former slaveholders had no intention of ending the class system based on race that had existed for more than a century. They quickly moved to ensure that freed blacks were kept in a state as close to slavery as possible. Various forms of voter suppression were enacted to prevent blacks from exercising their right to vote. Furthermore, the Ku Klux Klan carried out acts of terrorism against African Americans, often in the form of lynchings or beatings. Most blacks could only find work as tenant farmers or sharecroppers, positions that paid next to nothing and kept them tied to the same fields they had worked as slaves.

Black women working as nursemaids or domestic servants faced sexual violence at the hands of their employers and would lose their positions if they resisted. Jim Crow laws stifled blacks' rights during the late nineteenth century, and African Americans began fleeing the South. The numbers were small at first, as most blacks were too poor to travel, but began to increase during the twentieth century. Of course, blacks still faced racism in Northern cities. Many African Americans were forced to take work as strikebreakers (people who take work during a strike), as the racist hiring practices of Northern businessmen meant that blacks would often only be hired out of sheer desperation. For white workers in Chicago and other cities, black skin began to be associated with strikebreaking. Thus, class conflict combined with racial conflict to produce widespread acts of violence toward African Americans, and in some cases small-scale race riots.

The New Immigration

The growth of cities was largely driven by the massive amount of immigration in the late nineteenth and early twentieth centuries. Between 1880 and 1919, twenty-three million immigrants arrived on America's shores. Many were drawn by economic opportunity, hoping to make a better life for themselves in the United States than was possible in their countries of origin. Some had received letters from relatives already in America, urging them to make the two-week voyage across the Atlantic. Others were looking to avoid forced military service, while still others fled religious persecution. More than two million Jews came to the United States in this period, many fleeing violence directed toward them in Eastern Europe.

While previous waves of immigration had come mostly from Northern and Western Europe, the so-called new immigrants of this period originated primarily in Eastern and Southern Europe. The new immigrants were Italians, Poles, Greeks, Slovaks, and Jews, as opposed to the English, Irish, and German immigrants of previous generations. New immigrants were also less educated than the immigrants who came before them, had less experience with representative democracy, and belonged to non-Protestant faiths. Because of their lack of education and money, most new immigrants ended up living in large cities with other immigrants from their native countries. Little Italys or Little Polands, where traditions and customs of the old country continued to be practiced in the United States, emerged in various urban centers. New arrivals went to work in factories, sweatshops, and slaughterhouses, where they were exploited by their employers. Immigrants were worked twelve to fourteen hours a day, six days a week for starvation wages. They were also typically given the hardest labor in new industries. The bulk of the work on the railroads, for example, was done by Chinese and Irish immigrants, who died by the thousands laying rails and dynamiting mountains.

As had happened during the previous wave of immigration in the 1840s and 1850s, many native-born Americans reacted with hostility to the new arrivals. Workers had objections to immigrants working for lower wages or as strikebreakers. Most labor unions refused to accept immigrants out of a desire to protect jobs for Americans. Immigrants were also blamed for economic crises and were said to be taking up too many resources. They were the same objections that had been made against the Irish fifty years earlier and that would continue to

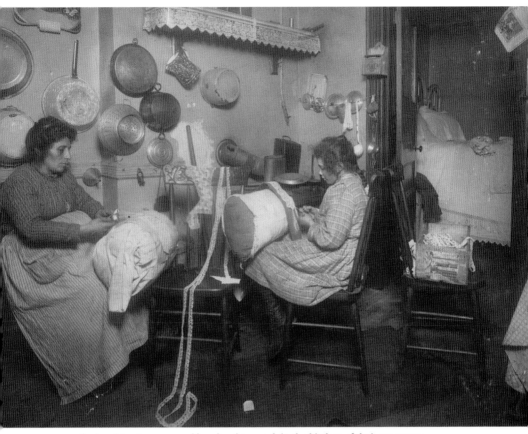

An immigrant woman and her daughter work in the kitchen of their tenement home in New York City.

be made against immigrants from all over the world for decades to come. Many nativists were particularly disturbed by the shift in the immigrants' country of origin. In 1882, 87 percent of immigrants came to the United States from Northern and Western Europe. By 1907, 81 percent of immigrants originated in Southern and Eastern Europe. Since these new immigrants had different customs, religions, and languages, they were seen as fundamentally un-American. Their presence was thought to be harmful to American institutions and traditions. This hostility toward the new immigrants only served to strengthen their communal bonds, as they were forced to rely on one another to survive in America. Immigrants formed their own unions, of Lithuanian meatpackers or Polish garment workers. Those who had lived in the country for some time helped new arrivals learn English. These efforts did little to halt the feeling of xenophobia among some Americans, but they did help ease the transition of later immigrants to life in the United States.

The Closing of the Frontier

At the same time that cities exploded in the East, Americans continued to stake out new settlements in the West. Discoveries of gold, silver, copper, and oil drew miners and prospectors out of eastern cities and to the boomtowns that had sprung up around quarries and oil wells. The Homestead Act of 1862, which offered settlers 160 acres (64.75 hectares) of western land at rock-bottom prices, also inspired many poor city-dwellers to try their luck on the frontier. Half a million families took advantage of this legislation over the forty years after its passage. Millions more purchased cheap land from the railroads, which were earning a tidy profit by selling the excess acreage they had been granted by the federal government. Many of these western tracts proved miserable and worthless, however. Up to two-thirds of homesteaders were forced to give up and return to the East. Despite such troubles, between 1865 and 1900, all of the lands west of the Mississippi River were settled and thoroughly transformed by white Americans. As usual, the victims of this settlement were the Natives, whose lands and lives were once again sacrificed.

In 1860, there were approximately 360,000 Natives living between California and the Mississippi, most of them on lands that had been set aside for exclusive tribal use in treaties. Over the next thirty years, those treaties would be ripped up one by one as settlers continued to invade Native land and claim it as their own. The federal government again declined to enforce treaty provisions, instead sending the military to protect the lives and property of white settlers. The Natives did attempt to fight back. Sitting Bull, Crazy Horse, and Red Cloud of the Sioux, Geronimo of the Apache, and Chief Joseph of the Nez Percé were just some of the many chieftains who led Native warriors in engagements with white soldiers and settlers.

Most Native attacks focused on military forts or railroads under construction and took the form of ambushes designed to harass the whites and draw them out into the open, where they could be more easily killed. The Natives had some important victories in these engagements. Red Cloud's War of 1866–1868 successfully halted the completion of a major road network. The Battle of the Little Bighorn in 1876 saw Lieutenant Colonel George Armstrong Custer and all the men under his command fall to a group of Sioux and Cheyenne led by Sitting Bull and Crazy Horse. But the triumphs were far outnumbered by the defeats. Villages were burned, and food supplies were destroyed. Massacres at Sand Creek, Colorado, and along the Washita River in present-day Oklahoma resulted in the deaths of hundreds of Native men, women, and children. The military had better weaponry, including access to artillery, and the new railroads brought in streams of fresh soldiers. Growing white settlements also drove off the herds of wildlife on which the Natives of the Plains depended for food, and the near-extinction of the buffalo (which declined in number from fifteen million in 1865 to fewer than a thousand by 1885) made hunger a major threat. The tribes were too spread out and too distrustful of one another to effectively unite in large numbers, and so the Natives began to surrender to the United States as starvation, disease, and warfare took their toll.

The survivors were herded onto reservations, many of which were located hundreds of miles from the tribes' homelands. Even these were not immune to white encroachment. When gold was discovered in the Black

Hills on the Great Sioux Reservation in 1874, the Sioux were coerced into signing away their claims to the land, the spiritual home of the tribe, under threat of forced starvation. The nomadic tribes of the Plains were especially unused to life in small, confined spaces, and suffered under the conditions. "Civilizing" initiatives, like those that had been forced on the Cherokees fifty years earlier, were also launched in an effort to "kill the Indian and save the man." In other words, the government sought to wipe out every unique, distinct aspect of Native culture and make the tribes indistinguishable from white Americans.

Tribal religious ceremonies were banned on the reservations, and individual Natives were given allotments of farmland in an effort to make them solitary planters, thereby breaking tribal bonds. Children were taken away from their parents without consent and sent to eastern boarding schools, where they were forced to dress like whites and speak only English and denied the opportunity to learn anything about the history or cultural practices of their people. Any efforts at resistance, even the entirely nonviolent Ghost Dance movement, were suppressed. The massacre at Wounded Knee Creek in December 1890, which claimed the lives of approximately two hundred cold, defenseless Natives, represented the final defeat of the Native Americans in the West.

Sioux corpses lie in the snow in the aftermath of the Wounded Knee massacre, in which hundreds of Native people were murdered by the US military.

In 1900, the Native American population of the United States stood at just 237,000 people. Depending on which pre-Columbus population estimate is used, this means that from 1500 to 1900, between 98 and 99 percent of the Native population of the Americas was destroyed through disease and/or warfare. The Native population began increasing again in the twentieth century, but the forced assimilation policies on the reservations continued until 1934. That's

American Migration and Settlement

When Chief Joseph, leader of the Nez Percé tribe of the Pacific Northwest, surrendered to the US military in 1877, he made a speech in English explaining the reasoning for his decision. He said, "Our chiefs are killed … The old men are all dead … it is cold and we have no blankets. The little children are freezing to death … Hear me, my chiefs! I am tired; my heart is sick and sad. From where the sun now stands I will fight no more forever."

Ouray the Arrow, a chief among the Ute of the Rocky Mountains, expressed the frustration felt by many Natives at the coercive nature of the supposedly fair treaties signed between Natives and white men. He said, "The agreement an Indian makes to a United States treaty is like the agreement a buffalo makes with his hunters when pierced with arrows. All he can do is lie down and give in."

Perhaps the simplest summation of the feelings of the Natives at the end of the nineteenth century was made by an anonymous member of the Lakota Sioux: "[The white Americans] made us many promises, more than I can remember, but they never kept but one; they promised to take our land, and they took it."

when the Indian Reorganization Act allowed the tribes to once again set up systems of self governance and preserve their ancestral crafts and traditions. (Native Americans had not been granted citizenship until 1924.) The supposedly protected Indian Territory, now the home of most of the relocated Natives from all of the Western territories, was opened to white settlement in 1889. Sixty thousand whites lived there by the end of the year. The white American population had now settled from coast to coast, and the frontier was closed.

The Quota System

The policies that had led to the destruction of the Native Americans also began influencing domestic immigration policy in the 1920s. Politics took a sharp turn to the right after World War I, resulting in a distrust of international alliances and foreigners. The Treaty of Versailles, which ended the war, was never ratified by the United States. Furthermore, the United States never joined the League of Nations, the forerunner of today's United Nations. The Bolshevik Revolution in Russia in 1917 prompted fears of similar political instability in the United States, leading to a series of raids against aliens accused of professing socialist or anarchist beliefs.

Nearly 250 aliens of Russian birth were deported to war-torn Russia in 1919. Another four thousand aliens were removed from the country in 1920. The most extreme example of this anti-foreign paranoia came with the execution of Nicola Sacco and Bartolomeo Vanzetti in 1927. The men were convicted of murder based less on the evidence in the case (which was extremely questionable) than on the fact that they were anarchists and Italians. The Ku Klux Klan saw a resurgence in the 1920s as well, boasting 4.5 million members in 1924. The organization was not only explicitly anti-African American, but also anti-Semitic, anticommunist, and anti-immigrant. The Klan was one of the loudest voices calling for restrictions on immigration. Fourteen million immigrants had come into the country between 1900 and 1920, mostly from Southern and Eastern Europe, but also from Mexico, which was undergoing a revolution. The fact that these immigrants were not white Anglo-Saxon Protestants infuriated not only the KKK but also many racist politicians. These politicians began drafting laws to deal with what they perceived as a crisis.

Before the late nineteenth century, the federal government played almost no role in regulating immigration. The president was empowered to deport "enemy aliens" in a time of war, but beyond that immigration laws were left to the individual states. As

Bartolomeo Vanzetti (*left*) and Nicola Sacco (*right*) were executed for murder in 1927. Their anarchist beliefs and Italian ancestry did more to convict them than did any actual evidence of their guilt.

immigration increased in the late nineteenth century, however, the federal government began exercising more oversight. Early laws prevented criminals, prostitutes, and anarchists from entering the country. In 1882, the Chinese Exclusion Act cut off all immigration from China, and the "Gentlemen's Agreement" of 1907 ended immigration from Japan. The Immigration Act of 1917 formalized these exclusions, declaring that no persons from East Asia would be allowed to immigrate to the country on a permanent basis and preventing Asians already in America from gaining citizenship. The law also established a literacy test in an attempt to keep out uneducated immigrants, most of whom were coming from Southern and Eastern Europe. The exclusionary efforts reached their height with the Emergency Quota Act of 1921 and the Immigration Act of 1924 (also known as the Johnson-Reed Act, after its sponsors). Building on earlier laws, the new legislation established a visa system that set quotas on how many immigrants could enter the United States from any given country. The quota for each nationality was set at 2 percent of the total number of people of that nationality present in the United States in the 1890 census.

In practice, this system effectively cut off immigration from Southern and Eastern Europe, while leaving Northern and Western Europe comparatively untouched. The new immigrants were only just arriving in 1890, while the

The first victims of America's exclusionary immigration policies were immigrants from China and Japan. Chinese immigrants had arrived first on the West Coast, lured by the gold rushes in California and the need for labor on the railroads. By 1880, there were seventy-five thousand Chinese immigrants in California, mostly poor, uneducated single men. They tended to live with other Chinese in districts that became known as Chinatowns, where they worked as cooks, laundrymen, or domestic servants. Thousands died while building the railroads. Thousands more saw their stores burned down or suffered beatings at the hands of white Americans. The Chinese were regarded as a threat to the economic livelihood of other California workers, particularly other immigrant workers, because of how little they were paid. In 1882, Congress passed the Chinese Exclusion Act, cutting off all immigration from China. The law was incorporated into the Immigration Act of 1924, and Chinese immigration remained illegal until 1943.

Japanese immigrants were better educated and mostly came as families, fleeing war and internal reforms in their home country. By the early 1900s, their numbers (seventy thousand Japanese had arrived by 1906) prompted fears among Californians of a "yellow menace," and Japanese students were banned from the state's schools. President

Chinese immigrants did much of the hardest work on the railroads of the American West before the passage of the Chinese Exclusion Act of 1882.

Theodore Roosevelt negotiated a "Gentlemen's Agreement" with the Japanese government over the course of 1907 and 1908. This resulted in Japan agreeing to prevent its citizens from immigrating to the United States, in exchange for better treatment of the Japanese already in California. As demonstrated by the internment of Japanese Americans during World War II, the United States did not hold up its end of the bargain.

immigrants of previous generations had been established in the country for far longer and in higher numbers by that point. As a result of the quota system, Italian immigration was capped at fewer than four thousand people per year, at a time when more than two hundred thousand Italians had been arriving on an annual basis. By contrast, more than 70 percent of the quota visas available were reserved for Great Britain, Ireland, and Germany, three countries that had stopped being major sources of immigration long before. Under the quota laws, only 165,000 total immigrants would be allowed to enter the country on a yearly basis. This was less than 20 percent of the pre–World War I average. Noncitizens found in the country without valid visas were now eligible to be deported. A border patrol was created to intercept immigrants attempting to enter the United States without authorization.

The bigotry of these restrictions did not go unnoticed. Michigan Congressman Robert H. Clancy made a speech against the law, in which he attacked the racial discrimination inherent in it. He also pointed out that the industrial boom undergone by the United States since the end of the Civil War had been driven in large part by immigration. New arrivals had laid the railroad tracks and worked for starvation wages in steel mills and garment factories. It was an objective fact that the country would have been far less prosperous if not for the massive numbers of immigrants. Supporters of the measure dismissed his objections, arguing that immigrants were lazy and taking up too many resources, which should be saved for natural population increases. They also used explicitly racial language, saying "unadulterated Anglo-Saxon stock" was the best in all the "Nordic breed." The laws had their desired effect. By 1931, more foreigners were leaving the country than arriving on an annual basis. The immigration tide that had brought thirty-five million people to the country's shores over the last century was stemmed. The nativists' desire to make the United States as white and Protestant as possible was being realized.

Terrible Consequences of the Quota System

The quota laws had their most disastrous effects during World War II. No provision was made in the laws for refugees or asylum seekers. As a result, Jews attempting to flee Europe in the 1930s and 1940s were turned away from America's borders. Anti-Semitism was so prevalent in the United States at the time that even a bill allowing German-Jewish *children* into the country above their quota was rejected by Congress. Nonquota admission was only granted to certain scholars, scientists, and artists. The most generous estimate of Jewish refugees allowed into the country during the rule of the Nazis (1933–1945) is 250,000, a tiny number when compared to the six

More than one hundred thousand Japanese Americans, most of them American citizens, were imprisoned in internment camps for three years during World War II.

million who were murdered in Europe. At the same time, 110,000 Japanese Americans were rounded up and interned in concentration camps along the West Coast for the duration of America's involvement in World War II. Following the Pearl Harbor attack on December 7, 1941,

American Migration and Settlement

fears of further violence combined with existing anti-Japanese racism to produce this bigoted policy. Two-thirds of those interned were American citizens. None had been proven guilty of anything in a court of law. Neither Italian Americans nor German Americans, also ethnically related to American enemies in the war, suffered anything close to this level of distrust or imprisonment. A congressional commission admitted the racism that motivated the policy in a 1983 report, and $20,000 in reparations were given to each surviving detainee. Though the policies that allowed for these shameful actions (and inactions) would change in the years after World War II, the attitudes behind them would remain remarkably similar.

Immigration reform activists have demonstrated regularly in support of immigrants' rights in recent decades.

Chapter Four

Modern Migrations: 1945 to Present

T he second half of the twentieth century saw new waves of immigration to the United States, as well as massive internal migrations. The Great Depression had sparked the first of these population shifts, in which 350,000 people moved from the Dust Bowl lands of Oklahoma and Arkansas to California in an effort to escape the dust storms that had ruined their farms. World War II then began what became essentially a constant migration of the population around the country for the next fifty years. The war sucked people into large cities, where they could find work in plants producing materials for the war effort. Los Angeles, Detroit, and Seattle all boomed during the war. The population of California grew by two million.

The Sunbelt and African American Migrations

After the war, rapid population growth was most noticeable in the Sunbelt region, the stretch of land across the southern half of the United States from Virginia to California. New industries in these regions drew in job seekers and their families, notably the electronics industry in California and the aerospace complexes in Texas and Florida. As federal policies made home ownership more affordable, and as newly built highways made it easier to commute longer distances to work, the suburbs began to bloom. Around 25 percent of Americans lived in suburbs in 1960. By the 1990s, suburbanites represented a majority of the country. A baby boom also took place in the twenty years after the end of the war. More than fifty million babies were born between 1945 and 1960, rapidly increasing the population.

One of the most significant internal migrations was that of African Americans. In 1910, 90 percent of the black population lived in the South under racist Jim Crow laws. Beginning with World War I, blacks began leaving the South and heading for Northern cities to find work in war plants. This migration exploded during World War II, when 1.6 million African Americans left the South. New technologies had eliminated much of the need for labor on Southern plantations, leaving large numbers of blacks

The development of Levittown on Long Island established a model of suburbia that would be copied throughout the United States during the 1950s and 1960s.

without a means of making a living. Since Southern war plants often refused to hire black workers, African Americans had no choice but to head to the North or West. The Great Migration continued after the war, as another five million blacks spread out across the country in the next three decades. By 1970, half of the country's black population lived outside of the South, and 80 percent lived in cities.

The migration of so many African Americans to Northern cities did not occur without incident. Racism existed throughout the country, and the sudden influx of large numbers of blacks into once majority white cities like St. Louis and Chicago provoked numerous race riots. It also led to the phenomenon of "white flight," whereby white city-dwellers moved to the suburbs to avoid having to live near racial minorities. Most blacks could not afford to buy houses, and those that could were often denied mortgages because of their race. The suburbs became largely white.

Advances and Retreats

The Native American population also migrated during the war, leaving the reservations for work in the cities or to serve in the army. In 1940, over 90 percent of the remaining Natives in the country lived on reservations. By 1980, nearly half lived in cities. This was in part the result of ongoing policies aimed at dispersing Natives throughout the country and further weakening their tribal bonds. The Relocation Act of 1956 had provided funds for job training for Natives in various cities but denied funds to establish similar programs on the reservations. Those that received this money were also typically required to sign agreements promising that they would not return to the reservations with their newly acquired skills.

A commission was established in 1946 to make cash settlements to various tribes for lands that were determined to have been acquired illegally. However, since the monetary awards were determined based on the value of the land at the time it was taken, the cash settlements were quite small. Therefore, the commission was more interested in giving the appearance of being fair and contrite than in actually offering meaningful reparation. Laws in the 1970s formally outlawed the practice of forcibly taking Native children to boarding schools and affirmed the rights of Natives to practice their religions. At the same time, Native efforts to fight for their rights and demand an improvement in their material conditions were met with repression.

Alcatraz Island was occupied by a group of Natives in 1969, and the village of Wounded Knee was occupied in 1973. The protests, designed to demand respect for Native land and rights, were harshly put down. Federal agents surrounded the Wounded Knee camp in an eerie echo of the massacre eighty-three years earlier. Anyone who attempted to get food to the Natives was arrested, and two of the occupiers were killed. The occupation eventually ended without mass violence, though nothing was done to address the Natives' demands.

A similar fate met the Native protestors at the Dakota Access Pipeline in 2017. The Sioux of the Standing Rock reservation peacefully protested the construction of an oil pipeline on sacred land and under their principal source of water for more than a year. They were joined by thousands of other demonstrators of all races. In response, police used pepper spray and water cannons to disperse the protesters, and the Trump administration gave final approval of the pipeline in February 2017. While public relations between the Natives and the federal government may have improved since 1945, there have been no meaningful

Russell Means, leader of the American Indian Movement, speaks during the occupation of Wounded Knee in 1973.

American Migration and Settlement

steps made to actually provide real redress or reparation to Native communities.

Native Americans face the most extreme poverty of any group in America. Unemployment remains rampant on the reservations (over 50 percent in some cases), and alcoholism and suicide rates are high. Native life expectancy is much lower than that of a white person of either gender. Despite this, the population has been steadily growing since its low point in 1900. Many ancestral beliefs and traditions have also been maintained. In the 2010 census, 2.9 million people identified as Native American, an increase of more than 2.5 million in the last century.

Immigration Reform

Aside from a few minor tweaks and the creation of a refugee admissions system in the wake of World War II, the quota-based immigration laws of the 1920s remained in place largely unchanged for forty years. As the civil rights movement prompted a broader examination of racist and discriminatory policies in the 1950s, however, the nation's immigration laws came under increased scrutiny. By the 1960s, calls for reform had resulted in a new piece of legislation, which continues to guide immigration policy today. The Immigration and Nationality Act of 1965 is also known as the Hart-Celler Act. It restructured the system of admissions to the United States, while also upholding some of the principles of the previous laws. Visas were now given out first to family members of immigrants already in the United States and then to skilled workers who could contribute to the American economy. Legal permanent residents could apply for citizenship after living continuously in the United States for five years, demonstrating "good moral character," and passing exams in English, history, and civics.

The new legislation did away with the racially based quotas but did not entirely do away with the idea of caps on immigration. In addition to a limit placed on total legal immigration (290,000 in 1965, currently 675,000), caps were also set on the number of immigrants admitted for employment purposes, as well as immigrants admitted from any one particular country. The per-country limit was initially set at 20,000 and has since been raised to 47,000. While this is a more neutral quota system than previously existed, it still works against the immigrants who need admission most urgently. The traditional causes of nonrefugee immigration (unemployment, poverty, and political instability) are felt more strongly in some countries than others. A poor country is going to produce more immigration than one that is economically and politically stable and will therefore require more visas. Denying those visas makes the immigration system biased

President Johnson on the Hart-Celler Act

Upon signing the Immigration and Nationality Act of 1965, President Lyndon Johnson made a short speech. In it, he pointed out the inequalities of the previous immigration law, remarking on the unfairness of the fact that "Only three countries were allowed to supply 70 percent of all the immigrants." He called the prior legislation "un-American" and vowed that the new law would better reflect the ideals of American democracy. He also reassured those skeptical of the new system that their fears of increased immigration fundamentally changing American society were largely unfounded. "This bill we will sign today is not a revolutionary bill," he said. "It does not affect the lives of millions. It will not reshape the structure of our daily lives, or really add importantly to either our wealth or our power."

President Lyndon Johnson signs the Immigration and Nationality Act of 1965 into law, restructuring the system of admissions to the United States.

toward immigrants from comparatively wealthy countries, who will be admitted despite a less pressing need. These comparatively wealthy immigrants will also most likely be white Europeans, meaning that even without explicitly racist quotas, the system is still set up to keep immigration from certain cultures in check. The diversity visa lottery system created in 1990 also demonstrates this problem. Designed for countries with low rates of immigration, fifty thousand visas are randomly given to applicants from countries that have produced fewer than fifty thousand immigrants in the previous five years. During the first three years of the program's existence, 40 percent of the visas went to Irish immigrants. By definition, the program benefits people from countries that are not producing large quantities of immigrants, leaving fewer options available for legal immigration from areas seeing mass population departures.

Between 1965 and 1995, more than eighteen million immigrants arrived in the United States, more than triple the number admitted during the previous thirty years. The largest number of immigrants (4.3 million) came from Mexico, while millions more came from the Philippines, Vietnam, Cuba, and the Korean peninsula. More than one hundred thousand people took advantage of the family reunification policies put in place. The principal source of immigration shifted from Europe to Asia and Latin

America. While half of all immigrants in the 1950s were from Europe, by the 1990s Europeans only accounted for 16 percent of total annual immigration. Asians represented 31 percent. Latino immigrants primarily clustered in the Southwest, and by 2000 accounted for one-third of the populations of Texas, Arizona, and California and half of the population of New Mexico. Mexican immigrants

The National Puerto Rican Day Parade in New York City is an annual celebration of the Puerto Rican community.

to these states primarily found work in the agricultural sector and visited their families back in Mexico whenever possible. There were also vibrant communities of Puerto Ricans in New York City and Cubans in Florida. As of 2015, Latinos represented 18 percent of the US population. Banding together, Latino immigrants and their descendants have not only become a powerful voting bloc but have also formed labor unions and community-based organizations to push for economic and political justice.

Undocumented Immigration

Prior to the quota laws, undocumented immigrants did not really even exist as a concept, since there was no extensive documentation required to enter the country. Those circumstances changed with the implementation of the visa system. Immigrants lacking valid authorization were now held to have entered the country unlawfully, and they could be deported by government officials.

Deportation policies were developed along the Southern border during the 1940s and 1950s, in concert with the *bracero* program. The *bracero* program began in 1942 as a way to supplement the loss of farm labor to the war effort in Europe and the Pacific. Mexican agricultural workers were brought across the border to work on vacant farms and harvest fruits and grains. Employers were required to pay a wage equal to that of American workers (though many did not) and provide transportation and living expenses. The program remained in place until 1964 and employed 4.6 million Mexicans during that time. The program also led to an increase in undocumented immigration. Many workers left the farms they had been taken to and sought higher-paid work elsewhere in the United States. Others were lured away from the program to states that were not legally allowed to participate in it, but nevertheless had employers willing to pay for cheap Mexican labor. As a result, a series of raids and deportations were launched by the US Border Patrol over the next decade to round up undocumented immigrants and return them to Mexico. Working in concert with Mexican authorities, American border patrol agents developed methods of raiding towns as efficiently as possible and processing thousands of immigrants for deportation in mere hours. The height of these deportation efforts came with the so-called Operation Wetback of 1954, in which one million undocumented immigrants, almost all from Mexico, were deported over the course of a year. ("Wetback" is a racial slur.)

Undocumented immigration did not stop there, however, and was, if anything, made worse by the shifts in immigration law in 1965. The quotas of the 1920s had not applied to immigrants from Latin America since so many businesses in the Southwest relied on cheap Mexican labor.

A Border Patrol inspector checks the documentation of a Mexican farmworker in 1951. Over a million Mexican laborers were deported during the 1950s.

Once country-specific caps were put in place, the number of Mexicans and other Latino immigrants that could be legally admitted to the country suddenly represented only

American Migration and Settlement

a tiny percentage of the total number either applying for admission or already present within the nation's borders. Nearly eight hundred thousand Mexicans were deported in the year following the implementation of these provisions, but the flow of immigration continued. Agribusinesses continued to pay for undocumented labor, and many Mexicans and other undocumented Latino immigrants did not have the luxury of waiting for legal admission. Throughout Central and South America, far more than twenty thousand (and today forty-seven thousand) people per country desired entry to the United States. For those living in areas of dangerous political and economic instability, waiting potentially years for legal admission was simply not possible.

The Immigration Reform Act of 1986 established penalties for employers who used undocumented labor, while also granting amnesty to three million undocumented immigrants already in the country. Further laws in the 1990s responded to frequent criticisms of undocumented immigrants. They were the same arguments that had been made many times before, and that had inspired the racist quota laws of the 1920s. Immigrants were blamed for taking jobs, using up too many of the nation's resources (in this case, receiving government benefits), and not assimilating quickly enough. In reality, the jobs disappearing during the 1990s were mostly being sent overseas or being eliminated entirely. Immigration had nothing to do with it. Studies also demonstrated that most undocumented immigrants worked miserable jobs that native-born Americans refused to take and collectively paid more in taxes than they received in benefits. Despite this, legislation was passed in 1996 under President Bill Clinton that increased border security, made deportations easier, and prevented any noncitizen (including legal immigrants that had not been in the country long enough to qualify for citizenship) from using social welfare programs.

Nevertheless, from 1990 to 2007, the undocumented population more than tripled, peaking at 12.2 million people. When Mexican immigration began to decline (one million fewer Mexican immigrants entered the country in 2012 than had entered in 2007, largely as a result of the global economic recession), the number of undocumented immigrants in the country plateaued at 11 million. Undocumented immigrants work in not only the agricultural sector, but in factories, restaurants, construction, and domestic labor positions.

State and local governments have continued to crack down harshly on the undocumented population, supported by the federal government. Many Southern states have passed laws blocking undocumented immigrants' access to housing, education, and employment. At the federal level, the creation of the Department of Homeland Security (DHS) and the assumption by the government of increased powers to detain noncitizens in the wake of the September 11, 2001, terrorist attacks have had increasingly negative effects on immigrant communities.

Immigration and enforcement functions have been assumed by DHS, particularly the organization known as ICE (Immigration and Customs Enforcement), which is mostly responsible for rounding up and deporting undocumented immigrants. This includes not only those immigrants caught at the Southern border but oftentimes immigrants who have lived in the United States for decades with their families and have broken no laws.

Refugee Admissions

Since 1980, refugees have been dealt with as a separate category of immigrant under US law. Refugees are defined as those unwilling or unable to return to their home countries owing to a "well-founded fear of persecution" of their race, religion, nationality, social group, or political opinion. Those applying for refugee status are required to undergo extensive interviews, screenings, and background checks. Each person must prove their individual need for refuge in the United States. Refugees can be excluded for medical, criminal, or security purposes, and the number of refugees admitted to the country in any given year is

Deriving their name from the Development, Relief, and Education for Alien Minors (DREAM) Act of 2001, the Dreamers are the two million undocumented young adults who were brought to the United States by their parents when they were children. Though they have grown up as Americans and have no real firsthand experience of their

Dreamers and other activists protest in support of undocumented immigrants in Washington, DC, in December 2017.

birth countries, the Dreamers are denied many of the basic privileges enjoyed by their peers. They cannot easily get a job, go to college, or even get a driver's license. Several different bills have been introduced in Congress attempting to establish a path for these young adults to follow to achieve legal citizenship. However, none have yet been enacted into law. Proponents argue that it is unfair to punish these children for the actions of their parents. They believe that denying Dreamers the opportunity to get an education or a job will only result in worse outcomes for both the Dreamers themselves as well as the larger communities in which they live.

In 2012, President Barack Obama introduced the Deferred Action for Childhood Arrivals (DACA) program, an executive order that allowed young adults between the ages of fifteen and thirty who had been brought to the United States as children to apply for deportation relief and a work permit. Though the program did not provide permanent legal status and had to be renewed every two years, it allowed more than eight hundred thousand young men and women to work lawfully, attend school, and live their lives without constant fear of deportation. On September 5, 2017, DACA was rescinded under the Trump administration, with no new applications or renewals of status accepted after March 5, 2018. In the face of this setback, Dreamer activists continue to fight for a path to legalization and citizenship not only for themselves, but for all undocumented immigrants.

determined by the president. Once a refugee has been accepted for resettlement in the United States, their request is transferred to the Refugee Processing Center. The center determines where the refugee will live and arranges for their travel. From start to finish, the process takes an average of eighteen to twenty-four months.

Refugees were produced in mass numbers during the Cold War, as millions of people around the world fled violence and dictatorial regimes. More than 750,000 Cubans arrived in the United States, especially Florida, between 1960 and 1990. The Vietnam War also produced hundreds of thousands of refugees. At the time of American withdrawal in 1975, 125,000 South Vietnamese associated with the United States were granted immediate admission. Half a million more followed in the ensuing years. Nearly 150,000 Cambodian refugees were also admitted to the country between 1975 and 1994, fleeing genocide under the Khmer Rouge and the chaos that followed the regime's removal from power. Refugees took mostly menial labor positions in assembly plants or restaurant kitchens and formed their own communities within larger cities.

Not all refugees were treated equally. American policy during the Cold War was driven by a desire to extend America's power over as much of the world as possible, as a check to the Soviet Union and the spread

Refugees from Vietnam represented a significant portion of the total refugees granted admission to the United States during the Cold War.

of communism. This was used as justification for dozens of military coups and rigged elections engineered by the American government around the world, as well as support for numerous dictators who were friendly to the United States. While the American government was eager to admit refugees from countries it designated as enemies (Cuba, China, Vietnam, and the Soviet satellite states in Eastern Europe, to name just a few), it was less keen on accepting those fleeing regimes with which it was allied. In order to admit refugees from Guatemala, El Salvador, Honduras, or any of the other Central and South American military dictatorships supported by the United States, the government would first have to admit that the regime in question was committing human rights abuses. Since this would prevent the United States from further arming and funding these dictators, it could not be done. The victims of these regimes were abandoned, left to either wait for admittance to the United States through one of the other means of obtaining visas, or to enter the country unlawfully.

A similar situation has taken place in recent times with refugees from the Middle East. Since the terrorist attacks of September 11, 2001, the number of refugees admitted to the United States has fallen dramatically. Over the same period, American invasions of Iraq and Afghanistan and military involvement in Libya and Syria have produced a refugee crisis of massive proportions. According to the UN Refugee Agency, there were more than 22 million refugees throughout the world in 2017, 5.5 million of them just from Syria. From the start of widespread violence in Syria in 2011 to the end of the 2016 fiscal year, however, the United States admitted just twelve thousand refugees from the country. Under President Barack Obama, total refugee admissions varied between seventy thousand and eighty-five thousand people per year. By contrast, in 1979, the United States admitted 111,000 Vietnamese refugees alone, and another 207,000 the year after. These totals from a single country dwarf the number of refugees admitted from the entire globe during the average year of the twenty-first century. This difference became even starker in 2017, when President Trump announced that he would not only halt the acceptance of Syrian refugees entirely but also put a stop to nearly all legal immigration from six different Muslim-majority countries (as well as North Korea and Venezuela).

The Future of Migration and Settlement

The United States has the world's largest immigrant population, and those numbers are only expected to increase in the years to come. Around fifty-nine million immigrants have come to the country since 1965, and today 14 percent of the nation's approximately 327 million people are foreign-born. Of those immigrants, 52 percent came from Latin America, and another 26 percent from Asia. Only 14 percent came from Europe. By contrast,

Europeans accounted for 84 percent of all immigration in 1960. This represents a shift in country of origin as significant as that of the late nineteenth century. The sheer number of immigrants over the last fifty years is higher than that in any previous wave of immigration. America's racial demographics have also shifted over the last half-century. As a proportion of the total population, whites have decreased from 84 percent to 62 percent between 1965 and 2015. Over the same period, the Latino population has increased from 4 percent to 18 percent, and the Asian American population has increased from less than 1 percent to 6 percent. The African American population has remained essentially the same, around 12 percent.

According to projections by the Pew Research Center, if current trends hold, new immigrants and their children will account for 88 percent of the population increase over the next fifty years. The foreign-born population of 2065 is expected to represent 17.7 percent of the total population, and more of those immigrants will come from Asia than Latin America. By 2065, Pew projects that the United States will not have a majority racial group. Whites will account for less than 50 percent of the population (46 percent, to be exact), Latinos will represent 24 percent, and Asian Americans will outnumber African Americans (14 percent to 13 percent).

It is unclear what effect the changing population will have on the nation's immigration laws. As immigrant communities grow and gain more influence in government, the media, and the private sector, it is to be hoped that the United States will become a place that finds strength in diversity.

★ CHRONOLOGY ★

1492 Christopher Columbus lands in the New World, bringing Europe into contact with the Americas.

1607 The first permanent English colony is founded at Jamestown, Virginia.

1619 Slaves are first brought into the American colonies.

1620 The Pilgrims arrive at Plymouth, Massachusetts, aboard the *Mayflower*.

1763 The Proclamation of 1763 prevents colonists from settling beyond the Appalachian Mountains.

1775–1783

The American Revolution is fought; the American colonies gain their independence and British territories west of the Appalachians at the end of the war.

1793 The invention of the cotton gin revolutionizes cotton production; the demand for slaves skyrockets.

1803 Thomas Jefferson makes the Louisiana Purchase.

1830   Andrew Jackson signs the Indian Removal Act.

1838–1839

The Trail of Tears results in the deaths of four
thousand Cherokee Natives during forced removal.

1840–1860

Peak of immigration from Ireland and Germany.

1845   Texas is annexed to the Union.

1846   A dispute over the Oregon Country is resolved with
Great Britain.

1848   Mexican Cession adds California and the Southwest
to the United States.

1861–1865

The American Civil War rages.

1882   The Chinese Exclusion Act bans Chinese
immigration to the United States.

1890–1920

Peak of new immigration from Southern and
Eastern Europe.

1890   The Wounded Knee Massacre ends Native resistance
in the West.

1907 A "Gentlemen's Agreement" cuts off Japanese immigration to the United States.

1924 The Immigration Act of 1924 sets quotas for admission to the United States that massively favor Northern and Western Europe; Native Americans granted American citizenship.

1934 Indian Reorganization Act recognizes Native tribes as legal entities.

1939–1945

World War II; the Great Migration of African Americans around the United States begins.

1942–1945

Over one hundred thousand Japanese Americans are detained in internment camps.

1945–1991

The Cold War between the United States and the Soviet Union plays a leading role in the creation of mass numbers of refugees around the world.

1954 Operation Wetback sees one million undocumented immigrants deported in a year.

1965 The Immigration and Nationality Act of 1965 dispenses with race-based quotas and restructures the American immigration system.

2001 Immigration enforcement transferred to Department of Homeland Security; America invades Afghanistan.

2012 President Barack Obama introduces the Deferred Action for Childhood Arrivals (DACA) program.

2017 The Trump administration announces a ban on immigration from eight nations and calls for a wall along the Southern border; the DACA program is terminated.

abolitionist A person who wants to eliminate slavery.

alien A resident of a country who is not a native of that country.

annexation The assumption of control over a region or territory that had previously been either self-governed or part of another state.

assimilation The process by which a member of one culture adapts to the traditions and customs of another.

bracero A manual laborer.

cession The voluntary surrender of land from one people or state to another.

colony A territory controlled by a state that is not formally a part of that state, either geographically or politically.

immigrant A person who moves from one sovereign country to another with the intention of settling permanently in the new country.

indentured servant A person who sells his or her labor to an employer for a fixed period of time, in exchange for basic necessities; indentured servants do not receive a traditional wage.

manifest destiny The belief that the United States was fated to expand across the entirety of North America and to spread its culture and ideals to the lands and peoples therein.

migrant A person who moves from one place to another, either temporarily or with the intention to settle in their new location.

nativist A person who believes in the promotion of the interests of a country's native-born population over those of its immigrant population; nativists typically seek restrictions on immigration and to limit the rights of immigrants within a country's borders.

popular sovereignty The belief that the people of a given society should have some degree of control over governmental decisions; in the American historical context, this concept is used specifically to refer to the belief that the local residents of a territory should have the ability to decide for themselves whether or not to allow slavery in that territory.

refugee An immigrant who is unable to live in his or her country of origin for fear of persecution due to his or her race, ethnicity, religion, nationality, social group, or political beliefs.

reservation An area of land set aside for and administered by a Native American tribe.

undocumented immigrant A permanent resident of a country who is not legally authorized to be in that country; undocumented immigrants may have entered the country unlawfully or stayed within its borders beyond the expiration of a temporary visa.

visa An authorization allowing a foreigner to enter, stay within, or permanently settle in a given country.

xenophobia Fear and distrust of people and things perceived as foreign.

★ FURTHER INFORMATION ★

Books

Brown, Dee. *Bury My Heart at Wounded Knee: An Indian History of the American West*. New York: Henry Holt and Company, 1970.

Katzman, David M., and William M. Tuttle, Jr., eds. *Plain Folk: The Life Stories of Undistinguished Americans*. Chicago: University of Illinois Press, 1982.

Ngai, Mae M. *Impossible Subjects: Illegal Aliens and the Making of Modern America*. Princeton, NJ: Princeton University Press, 2004.

Ziegler-McPherson, Christina A. *Selling America: Immigration Promotion and the Settlement of the American Continent, 1607–1914*. Santa Barbara, CA: Praeger, 2017.

Websites

The American Immigration Council

https://www.americanimmigrationcouncil.org

The AIC is a nonprofit organization dedicated to defending immigrants' rights, and its website contains a wealth of information on American immigration laws, how they came about, and how they are enforced.

The Statue of Liberty – Ellis Island Foundation, Inc.

https://www.libertyellisfoundation.org

The website of the foundation dedicated to preserving Ellis Island and the Statue of Liberty boasts not only extensive discussions of the history of Ellis Island during the late nineteenth and early twentieth centuries, but also a searchable database of the immigrants who passed through the station, potentially allowing visitors to learn more about their own ancestors.

UNHCR: The UN Refugee Agency

http://www.unhcr.org/en-us

The UN Refugee Agency's site features extensive discussions of the many refugee crises in the world today, along with statistics, images, and ways you can help.

Videos

Human Flow (2017)

Available on Blu-ray and DVD

Directed by Ai Weiwei, this haunting documentary focuses on the global refugee crisis, highlighting the challenges faced and sacrifices made by those fleeing their homes and seeking a better life for themselves and their families.

"The Middle Passage"

https://www.history.com/topics/black-history/
slavery/videos/the-middle-passage?m=528e3
94da93ae&s=undefined&f=2&free=false

This short video discusses the traumas endured by Africans during their involuntary transport to the New World; links to further videos on the history of slavery in America are also provided.

★ BIBLIOGRAPHY ★

Bailey, Thomas A., David M. Kennedy, and Lizabeth Cohen. *The American Pageant: A History of the Republic.* 11th ed. Boston: Houghton Mifflin, 1998.

Cozzens, Peter. *The Earth is Weeping: The Epic Story of the Indian Wars for the American West.* New York: Alfred A. Knopf, 2016.

Hernández, Kelly Lytle. "The Crimes and Consequences of Illegal Immigration: A Cross-Border Examination of Operation Wetback, 1943 to 1954." *The Western Historical Quarterly* 37, no. 4 (Winter 2006). http://www.jstor.org.

History Matters. "'Shut the Door': A Senator Speaks for Immigration Restriction." Retrieved February 27, 2018. http://historymatters.gmu.edu/d/5080.

———. "An 'Un-American Bill': A Congressman Denounces Immigration Quotas." Retrieved February 27, 2018. http://historymatters.gmu.edu/d/5079.

Jaimes, M. Annette, ed. *The State of Native America: Genocide, Colonization, and Resistance.* Boston: South End Press, 1992.

Lemay, Michael, and Elliott Robert Barkan, eds. *U.S. Immigration and Naturalization Laws and Issues: A Documentary History*. Westport, CT: Greenwood Press, 1999.

Liptak, Adam. "Supreme Court Allows Trump Travel Ban to Take Effect." *New York Times*, December 4, 2017. https://www.nytimes.com/2017/12/04/us/politics/trump-travel-ban-supreme-court.html.

Pew Research Center. "Modern Immigration Wave Brings 59 Million to U.S., Driving Population Growth and Change Through 2065: View of Immigration's Impact on U.S. Society Mixed." September 28, 2015. http://www.pewhispanic.org/2015/09/28/modern-immigration-wave-brings-59-million-to-u-s-driving-population-growth-and-change-through-2065.

Starkey, Armstrong. *European and Native American Warfare, 1675–1815*. London, UK: UCL Press, 1998.

Thornton, John. *Africa and Africans in the Making of the Atlantic World, 1400–1800*. Second edition. Cambridge, UK: Cambridge University Press, 1998.

Thornton, Russell. *American Indian Holocaust and Survival: A Population History Since 1492*. Norman, OK: University of Oklahoma Press, 1987.

Volpp, Leti. "Impossible Subjects: Illegal Aliens and Alien Citizens." *Michigan Law Review* 1595 (May 2005). https://scholarship.law.berkeley.edu/cgi/viewcontent.cgi?article=1013&context=facpubs.

Zinn, Howard. *A People's History of the United States*. New York: HarperCollins Publishers, 2005.

★ INDEX ★

Europeans, 6–9, 11, 14, 16, 20–21, 80–81, 94

freedom dues, 14, 19

gold, 6–7, 10–11, 21, 39, 42, 54, 56, 64

Hart-Celler Act, 77, 79
Homestead Act of 1862, 54

immigrant, 31–32, **46**, 48, 51–54, **53**, 61, 63–64, 66–67, 78–87, 89, 93–95
Immigration and Customs Enforcement (ICE), 87
Immigration and Nationality Act, 77, 79, **79**
Inca civilization, 21
indentured servant, 14–15, **15**, 18–19
Indian Removal Act, 39
Industrial Revolution, 48
internment camps, 65, 68–69, **68**

Jackson, Andrew, 28, 36–39, **36**
Jamestown colony, 10–11, **10**, 22
Jews, 13, 51, 67
Jim Crow laws, 50, 72
Johnson, President Lyndon, 79, **79**

Kansas and Nebraska Acts, 42
Know-Nothing Party, 32
Ku Klux Klan (KKK), 50, 61

Latinos, 82, 94
Louisiana Purchase, **26**, 28

manifest destiny, 28–29, 45
Mexican Cession, 30, 41–42
migrant, 49
Missouri Compromise, 41, 43

Native Americans, 5–9, **10**, 11, 13, 16, 20–25, 27–28, 32, 34–39, 55–60, 74–77
Native slavery, 7, 13, 16, 21

★ ABOUT THE AUTHOR ★

★ ★ ★ ★ ★ ★ ★

Brett Griffin earned a degree in history from Canisius College, with a focus on American and European history. Other books written by Griffin include *The Interwar Years: Weimar Germany and the Rise of Fascism* and *History Makers: Sitting Bull: Native American Leader*. In addition to history, Griffin is passionate about film, music, and literature and enjoys pursuing those interests in his spare time. He lives in Buffalo, New York.

★ ★ ★ ★ ★ ★ ★